Called to the bar in 2012, Alex Matthews is a specialist criminal barrister at 9BR Chambers.

She acts for both prosecution and defence across a wide range of cases such as sexual offences, firearms, explosives and serious violence through to fraud.

Alex has particular experience representing vulnerable clients within the criminal justice system from youths to those with severe mental ill health. Through this experience she developed an interest in the law of this area both in its current form, and in relation to its proposed reform.

As part of her specialism in protest law Alex has dealt extensively with the complex law in that area and has a consequence also been published in Archbold Review.

Having been appointed both to the Criminal Bar Association and South Eastern Circuit committees (the latter as the Recorder of the South Eastern Circuit) Alex is an active participant in circuit life.

Alex is a Rape and Sexual Offences panel prosecutor and an established grade 3 advocate for the Crown Prosecution Service.

A Practical Guide to Fitness to Plead and Insanity in the Crown Court and Magistrates Court

A Practical Guide to Fitness to Plead and Insanity in the Crown Court and Magistrates Court

Alex Matthews

Barrister

9BR Chambers

Law Brief Publishing

Published 2023 by Law Brief Publishing, an imprint of Law Brief Publishing Ltd
30 The Parks
Minehead
Somerset
TA24 8BT

www.lawbriefpublishing.com

Paperback: 978-1-916698-02-4

PREFACE

In writing this book my aim is that it is literally a 'practical guide'; useful to a criminal advocate presented with a client who appears to be suffering from mental ill health either at the time of an offence, or when before the court. Given it is a 'practical guide', discussion of changes in law or esoteric musings on whether the law is fit for purpose are limited.

So too, as a practical guide, some of the terms from the relevant acts are adopted. These are terms which are to a modern ear outdated and are terms not used in modern psychiatry. As someone who works very frequently with those with acute mental disorders, and/or learning and cognitive difficulties, often facing the most serious of charges, I am acutely aware of the disempowerment of those suffering mental ill health within the justice system and the tendency the system has to 'categorise' and deprive many of a voice.

At no point do I seek to follow that trend by adopting the language which is inherently part of the system. The antiquated language is adopted here with the express aim of speaking in simple language which focuses on the law as it stands.

Mental health has been systematically defunded; care in the community is now well established but it is also fundamentally apparent that there is no resource for that care. Police have even begun to refuse to attend when 'no crime' is reported but someone is suffering a mental health event. In this landscape the criminal justice system is where those suffering crisis often end up, quite frequently through no fault of their own.

Criminal advocates are not usually experts in psychiatry, albeit we have extensive experience of the human condition playing out before us in court and in conference. Because of the lack of specific expertise in the medial sense, the provision of a quick reference text is the aim.

I will make reference to some of the mental health defences available in certain circumstances, but this is not intended to compendiously address defences such as 'diminished responsibility' or automatism; many books would be required to full address the same. That being said, I hope to sign post when it might be that such offences crop up, and the path an advocate ought take when looking toward dealing with the same.

My thanks to Rebecca Steels at 9BR Chambers for her help regarding the magistrates' court. The regime is so desperately lacking that practical examples are very helpful when it comes to dealing with the actual implementation of the legislation and case law in this area and hers has been invaluable.

The quoted law was believed to be accurate as of the 10th October 2023.

Alex Matthews
October 2023

CONTENTS

CHAPTER ONE

INFORMATION GATHERING

Following the order in which one might encounter a mentally vulnerable defendant, it makes sense to begin at the beginning when an advocate first encounters a defendant.

This section aims to address:

- Information the advocate needs to gather

- Taking initial instructions

Whenever representing a defendant an advocate will of course have an eye to their mental wellbeing. It may be, having the good fortune of having been instructed in advance and armed with psychiatric record and reports, the advocate is well prepared and knows full well their client's condition. However, too often one arrives at the door of court with merely a case summary and an antecedent record. In such circumstances information gathering is the first order of business.

Some information relates to the facts of the case on the face of the papers and from those personnel at court. Things to look out for might include:

- Out of character behaviour – a defendant of previous positive good character suddenly lashing out violently or performing a sexual act in public;

- Friends or family can provide anecdotal details ie 'he was sectioned a month ago', which can help assess the lay of the land:

- Is there a liaison and diversion service at court – can they assist with any information or a brief assessment;

- Was there an appropriate adult in interview;

- Is the FME's attendance apparent and available for review;

- Experienced officers may note mental health factors in their statements or case summaries.

So too, the client's presentation and initial instruction is key to your assessment:

- Does the defendant have missing periods of recollection without the intervention of drugs and alcohol;

- Is their presentation to you disordered, muddled or volatile (again, as far as you can tell not due to drugs or alcohol)

No advocate is required at court to 'diagnose' a defendant; a lawyer's expertise is in the law, not in medicine or psychiatry. However, those working in criminal courts are put in the unenviable position of needing to make an initial assessment as regards whether there are potential mental health issues which may require expert assessment. We are often tasked with doing so rapidly and without the support of any sort of intervention service.

Without wishing to pretend to expertise I do not have (I am in no way medically qualified) it is always the case that an advocate will need to be alert for a client presenting in psychosis. This can present itself in many ways. For the advocate in conference things to look out for include:

- Hallucinations – seeing, hearing, smelling, tasting or feeling things that are not happening
- Delusions – ie beliefs that the person is in a position of power, or that people are planning to hurt them
- Confused thought patterns – speaking quickly, abrupt topic changes, sudden switches mid-sentence.

The above are a beginning of the ways an advocate might start to assess a client is giving instructions, if they are capable of doing so at that juncture, and whether there are mental health issues or disorders in play, importantly either at the time of the offence or on the date on which the defendant has arrived at court.

The defendant may be suffering acute mental health issues in police or court custody and often may not adhere to societal norms or keep hold of their temper or fear. A key issue for the advocate will be ensuring the court does not rush proceedings and is aware of the issues at hand.

It is in this context that the issues of insanity and fitness to plead can begin to be considered; only when information has been gathered can the application of the various statutory regimes begin.

CHAPTER TWO

THE MAGISTRATES' COURT

Essential Reading

- R (P) v Barking Youth Court [2002] EWHC Admin 734
- s37(3) Mental Health Act 1983; and
- s11(1) Power of Criminal Courts (Sentencing) Act 2000.

Introduction

There are crucial and somewhat arbitrary differences between the Crown Court and magistrates' court when it comes to fitness to plead procedures.

The scheme addressed in this book relating to the Crown Court falls under the Criminal Procedure (Insanity) Act 1964. Of note this *only* applies in the Crown Court.

Conversely, in the youth and magistrates' courts (referred here collectively as the magistrates' court unless otherwise specified) this statutory procedure does not exist.

As a result the court is left with a hodgepodge approximation of a fitness to plead regime in the lower courts which has significant 'holes' in it.

The measures frankly do not meet the needs of defendants, particularly vulnerable youths who can face very serious charges such as rape in the Youth Courts, and indeed present with significant vulnerabilities (those difficulties often being the reason they are before the court in the first place) without the protections that the Crown Court scheme affords.

What then, is in place in the magistrates' courts?

The "Statutory Regime"

As per *R (P) v Barking Youth Court* [2002] EWHC Admin 734 the High Court set out the framework for dealing with issues of fitness to plead in the lower courts (both Youth and magistrates').

Essentially it is a combination of:

- s37(3) Mental Health Act 1983; and
- s11(1) Power of Criminal Courts (Sentencing) Act 2000.

37(3) Mental Health Act 1983 states:

> *"Where a person is charged before a magistrates' court with any act or omission as an offence and the court would have power, on convicting him of that offence to make a Hospital or Guardianship order under subsection (1) above in his case as being a person suffering from mental illness or severe mental impairment, then if the court is satisfied that the accused did the act or made the omission charged, the court may, if it thinks fit, make such an order without convicting him."*

In turn:

Section 11(1) PCC(S)A 2000 states:

> *"If, on the trial by a magistrates' court of an offence punishable on summary conviction with imprisonment, the court—*
>
> *a) is satisfied that the accused did the act or made the omission charged, but*
>
> *b) is of the opinion that an inquiry ought to be made into his physical or mental condition before the method of dealing with him is determined,*
>
> *the court shall adjourn the case to enable a medical examination and report to be made, and shall remand him".*

"Remand"

A remand is either for three weeks in custody or four weeks if on bail (section 11(2) PCC(S)A 2000).

Those representing defendants ought keep in mind the possibility that if remanded into custody they can be transferred to a hospital environment under the auspices of s.48 Mental Health Act 1983.

If the defendant is indeed in custody, the above time-span of '3 weeks' leaves scant time for a mental health report to be prepared and repeated hearings and adjournments are to be anticipated. Information gathering and ensuring an advocate is equipped with all the historic reports in existence is key in this scenario.

Problems with the Regime

"Mental Disorder"

The eagle eyed will note from the framing of the statute one issue becomes immediately apparent; this statutory framework only applies to defendants with a "mental disorder".

Defendants who have learning difficulties or communication problems and/or problems with memory do not necessarily fall under this head, and yet they are naturally much less able to comprehend the process of court proceedings.

The focus is on a 'disorder' not capacity in real terms; if a defendant does not have a diagnosis which fits within this rather restrictive rubric, the scheme cannot assist him.

Imprisonable Only

So too, this procedure only applies to "imprisonable" offences. Thus, if charged with a summary only matter for which the punishment is fines, there is absolutely no recourse to any form of fitness to plead procedure.

A prime example of this would be s.5 Public Order Act "threatening or abusive words or behaviour", an offence which it is all too easy to stray towards if suffering mental illness.

It may be that the rationale for this is that fines only matters are of such low import in the justice system as a whole that they do not merit the protections afforded to imprisonable matters. This is a weak rationale however and it is hard to see how it remains Article 6 (right to fair trial) compliant when ultimately someone is unable to understand the charges they face, and could end up with a conviction when having never understood any part of the process.

This is of course compounded by the fact that many defendants in the magistrates' courts remain unrepresented.

Ultimately the situation is, in this author's view, entirely without logic and deeply unsatisfactory.

Focus on Disposal

Another significant issue with the regime is also the focus on the disposal before there is any sort of focus on the actual facts of the matter at hand; the entire drive of the above legislation places the focus on how the case ought be disposed of.

This rather puts the "cart before the horse" almost framing the "trial of the act" as a mere aside with the focus on the ability of the court to make hospital orders (more on which below).

Limited Disposals

Moreover, where, if convicted at trial it seems likely the defendant would receive a suspended sentence with mental health treatment requirement, there is a perverse incentive by which in the short term the "better" course might seem to ensure the defendant is convicted of an offence, so the help that is needed can be secured. In the long term however, the defendant has a conviction on his record and is not afforded the protection to his potential good character that a fitness to plead procedure would offer; a mere finding that he "did the act" differs greatly from a finding he committed an offence but in order to secure the best "result" for him, it may be that advocates feel pushed into ensuring he is not trammelled into the magistrates' inefficient and insufficient fitness to plead provisions.

Allocation and Plea before Venue

The above statutory regime also does not quite make room for the fact that the defendant may arrive at the first appearance apparently quite unwell and without capacity to instruct.

In the case of a defendant facing an *imprisonable* summary only charge things are relatively simple; as per the below the court will likely adjourn for reports before embarking on a trial, or a trial of the act. This process is explained in more detail below.

So too, indictable only matters are relatively simple; the Crown Court must try the case. The defendant can make no indication as to plea. It may behove the advocate at this stage to make plain that there are clear mental health issues and reports are required, but the necessity for instructions and participation from a defendant are limited. So, hopefully, no supervening issues occur here.

In the case of a defendant only facing summary only *non-imprisonable* matters, things become slightly more thorny; there is no fitness to plead procedure in place at all.

If a lack of capacity and wellbeing is so clear it may be that the prosecution can be prevailed upon to review the prosecution entirely. The level of charge being low there is some prospect of successful review.

Failing that, and addressed in some detail below, it may be the defence have to resort to an application to stay the matter as an abuse of process there being absolutely no provision for defendants in such circumstances.

What however, if the defendant faces "triable either way" charges? As will become apparent throughout this chapter, the Crown Court regime is significantly more robust and able to meet the needs of vulnerable defendants; often it is desirable, if the defendant is remotely capable of instructing, for the defendant to elect Crown Court trial, or the magistrates to decline jurisdiction and send the matter up to the Crown Court in order to provide the additional protection this affords to the defendant.

A case dealing with this issue was *Lincoln (Kesteven) Magistrates Court* [1983] 1 All E.R. 901. The defendant was not fit to even participate in allocation. The justices in that case, under the predecessor to s.37 Mental Health Act 1983, were put to considering whether they had the power to deal with a defendant who could not participate at all. They found they could deal with him by way of a hospital order and thus were able to proceed even though he was not able to participate in this part of proceedings.

It was emphasised how rare such a situation would be, however in this case, and in the slightly later case of R. v Ramsgate JJ Ex p. Kazmarek, 80 Cr. App. R. 366 the principle seems to be established that the magistrates' court can proceed on to an actus reus trial, even if the defendant is not capable of participating in plea before venue.

Of note however, a youth charged with triable either way matters is at a real disadvantage as there are very restricted circumstances when they might elect Crown Court trial.

R(P) v Derby Youth Court [2015] EWHC 573 (Admin), (2015) 179 JP 139 held it was not appropriate to send a child or young person who was "unfit to plead" to the Crown Court for trial under the Crime and Disorder Act 1998, s 51A(3)(b).

The reasoning for this was due to being "unfit," the youth defendant could not be "found guilty". By analogy this too applies to section 51A(3)(d), the power by which he would be sent. Thus, youths are at a particular disadvantage as regards venue.

Where the prosecution continues in spite of this, and there are very real difficulties with the youth participating in proceedings, there remains only the power of stay (addressed below).

Special Measures

Before resorting to fitness to plead measures (which presume an inability to instruct, and therefore to an extent prevent the accused's participation in his trial) a key area for advocates to be aware of is the ability of special measures to render a defendant "fit to plead" when s/he might otherwise not be.

In the Crown Court as much as the lower courts, advocates ought canvass the possibility of instructing an intermediary throughout.

Alternatively, advocates might note that under section 33B Youth Justice and Criminal Evidence Act 1999 (inserted by section 47 of the Police and Justice Act 2006) a live link can make it more feasible for a defendant to participate in proceedings. While this subsection is specifically directed at defendants over 18 and suffering from a mental disorder, s.33A(4) makes the same provision for youths; if their participation in proceedings might be improved by a link, this option ought be considered.

Procedure: Summary Only Trial

Should the case be summary only and imprisonable, the Court must embark on the statutory regime as per the *Barking Youth Court* case (amongst others)[1]. This is a 'flexible framework' to be adapted to the needs of each case.

By way of a suggested order of business, using *Barking Youth Court* as a guide the following seems to be the most sensible way of applying the scant statutory guidance available:

1. Issues relating to unfitness to plead must be raised at the start of proceedings, or as soon as they are apparent;

2. Defence provide written or oral evidence of two registered medical practitioners that the defendant has a mental disorder requiring treatment;

3. Prosecution review case or instruct experts themselves;

4. A criminal trial or 'fact finding' actus reus hearing;

5. If found to have committed the act, possibly adjournment for further medical evidence; or, if found not to have committed the act, then a 'not guilty' verdict is recorded.

---

1 *R (P) v Barking Youth Court* [2002] EWHC 734 (Admin), [2002] 2 Cr App R 19; *Lincoln (Kesteven) Justices* [1983] 1 WLR 335, [1983] 1 All ER 901; *R (Singh) v Stratford Magistrates' Court* [2007] EWHC 1582 (Admin), [2007] 1 WLR 3119; and *Blouet v Bath and Wansdyke Magistrates' Court* [2009] EWHC 759 (Admin), [2009] MHLR 71.

The above is supported by various cases which, while acknowledging that the framework only truly requires medical evidence relating to disposal, indicate that case management requires medical evidence much earlier. *Blouet v Bath & Wansdyke Magistrates' Court* [2009] EWHC 759 (Admin) is one case in which the need for the court to be provided with "up to date" medical information was emphasised.

Trial of the Act in the Magistrates' Court: The Hearing

The nature of the trial of an act is addressed in the Crown Court section of this book; in essence it is a trial of the "actus reus". The court will look to establish whether the defendant did the act or made the omission alleged against him.

Of note, the hearing may, if there are already psychiatric reports in existence (or the court has adjourned for them) be listed as specifically an actus reus hearing. It is also possible for a trial to transmogrify into a fact-finding enquiry part way through. (CPS v P [2007] EWHC 946 (Admin)).

No enquiry into the mens rea element of the offence is required in an actus reus hearing in the Crown Court, but again that remains somewhat undefined in relation to the magistrates' court; it would seem that the Crown Court case law must apply here but there is by no means any 'bright line' of authority paving the way.

One key area in issue is that in the Crown Court as per the case of *Antoine* [2001] 1 AC 340 if there is evidence on the face of the Crown's case of a potential defence (ie in an assault case, there is some evidence of self-defence or accident) the Crown need to negative that defence in an actus reus trial. The jury is directed accordingly that they must consider the "objective" evidence of such a defence, and establish for themselves whether it operates on these facts.

In an actus reus trial in the magistrates' court, does that also apply? There is no authority on the proposition (and indeed most of the authority in this area is cobbled together from various cases which do not necessarily all 'gel').

Thus, an advocate is left grasping at straws and analogies to Crown Court procedures to find the answers. Certainly out of fairness to a defendant the magistrates' court ought, in this author's view, have regard to the Court of Appeal authority if this were to be a live issue in an actus reus hearing. However, the lack of clarity on this point just goes to demonstrate the lacking nature of the regime in general terms and the need for reform.

What does appear clear is that the "finding of the act" must be done in accordance with normal rules of evidence; the Crown must call evidence in line with usual hearsay and bad character provisions, and call either witnesses or evidence admitted subject to s.9 or s.10 as per any other trial. (R (Singh) v Stratford Magistrates' Court [2007] EWHC 1582 (Admin), [2007] 1 WLR 3119, [35]; Lincoln (Kesteven) Justices [1983] 1 WLR 335, [1983] 1 All ER 901).

Disposals upon finding of the act

The only disposals are a "hospital order" (without restriction) or "guardianship order".

Unlike in the Crown court, an absolute discharge is not available to the court. This is deeply unequal and about-face as the opportunity for the defendant to receive a disposal which does not appear on his record is only available in the higher court, for arguably more serious matters; in the lesser court in relation to less serious cases this is not available to the bench. Again, the area needs reform.

So too a supervision order is available to the Crown Court but not the lower courts. Again, this is inverse to the potential severity of the charges in each venue. Again, it makes little sense.

Even in the Crown court the number of supervision orders made is increasingly limited, in line with increasingly scarce resources, but to restrict the magistrates' court from the ability to make such an order seems unduly limiting, and to a degree, perverse.

Hospital Orders (The Making Of)

The making of hospital orders under s.37 is explored more fully in the Crown Court section of this book and the statute and conditions precedent for their making are listed there.

Although a restriction order is not available in the magistrates' court, nonetheless, a finding of fact may result in indefinite hospitalisation so these are swinging powers to grant a lay bench.

Interim orders under s.38 are also available while the court considers making such an order. These should be for a period not exceeding twelve weeks and may be further renewed thereafter for 28-day periods, subject to an overall maximum period of twelve months while the court obtains and considers expert evidence.

Whilst magistrates' courts do have the power to commit in many cases if they are concerned that a hospital order with restriction is required under s.41 MHA, it is key to note that they do not have such a power within these proceedings if there has merely been a finding of the act.

Guardianship Orders

Guardianship orders are available in remarkably similar circumstances to a hospital order and essentially the offender is placed under the guardianship of local social services or an approved person and are also governed under s.37 MHA.

The local authority, if an order is made, allow for it to determine place of residence, require attendance for treatment, occupation, education or training, and to require access to the patient in any place of residence for a doctor, social worker or other specified person.

As per s.37(6) the order cannot be made unless the local authority, or person named as an appropriate guardian, is willing to receive the offender into guardianship.

Section 39A empowers a court which is minded to make a guardianship order to request the local social services authority to inform the court whether it would be willing to comply with the order and, if so, to give information about how it would exercise its powers under s. 40(2).

They last for 6 months but can be renewed upon application.

Of note they are only available to those over 16, and of course they depend on the availability of resources to a significant extent – the absence of a suitable "guardian" will mean the order is unavailable, and, as with hospital orders, they are only available to those suffering from a "mental disorder".

This is therefore another area in which the limitations on disposals under section 37(3) of the MHA are even more problematic. For defendants aged under 16, the only disposal available under section 37(3) of the MHA is a hospital order. This is rarely the most suitable option for a teenager in the justice system, nor suited to tackle offending behaviour. This is another aspect of the way in which the system fails those facing the youth justice system.

Abuse of Process and Stays

The vexed question of what to do when neither of the disposals are viable again demonstrates the deficiencies of the current regime.

If, for example, two up to date psychiatric reports indicate that a hospital order is not warranted, and that guardianship is not suitable either (or there is no one available to act as guardian), the court must proceed to a trial of the defendant as it cannot properly proceed to an actus reus hearing; there is no resolution available to it if it does have a trial of the act.

So too, the issue of youths who are unable to elect Crown Court trial and are therefore unable to participate in their trial in the youth court remains unresolved.

In both sets of circumstances the first port of call ought be prevailing upon the prosecution to discontinue the case. This is a difficult proposition; if the case has been properly reviewed before institution there will be both evidence and a public interest in the case being tried. In those cases the youth court deals with, these cases are often very serious and the public interest in their being tried is high. The Crown are therefore not always amenable to the sentiment that their prosecution ought be reviewed and dropped, especially if they do not place much 'store' in particular defence experts, or perhaps if they consider the issue to have been "over-egged" by the defence.

Conversely, the defence may be stuck in limbo with a defendant who is unable to participate in proceedings and deemed "unfit" by experts, but still facing a trial as there is no other route the magistrates' court can take due to the limitations on disposal. Another possible version is that the actus reus trial has been heard, but revised medical reports indicate that a hospital order is no longer warranted (mental health does after all fluctuate). In this situation the defence are left with a case potentially left suspended in mid-air with no resolution available; it is inimical to justice for a defendant to be left in the position of facing proceedings without end.

The only remaining route available, if the prosecution seek to continue the case, is to seek to stay the proceedings as an abuse of process.

Such an application invites the court to stay the proceedings on the basis that it will be impossible, as a result of the defendant's participatory difficulties, for him or her to have a fair trial (*Connelly v DPP* [1964] AC 1254, [1964] 2 WLR 1145 and *DPP v Humphrys* [1977] AC 1, [1976] 2 WLR 857).

The power to stay as an abuse of process is, as in other cases, "sparingly used" (Horseferry Road Magistrates' Court ex parte Bennett [1994] 1 AC 42).

The power be employed only in "exceptional circumstances" R (Ebrahim) v Feltham Magistrates' Court [2001] EWHC Admin 130.

Of note this is even more restricted when one contemplates youth proceedings in which it is clear the court is very likely to hear evidence before any such decision is contemplated (*R(TP) v West London Youth Court* [2005] EWHC 2583 (Admin))

There are always two limbs under which one can "run" an abuse of process argument. Sir Brian Leveson P summarised these in *Crawley* [2014] EWCA Crim 1028, [2014] 2 Cr App R 16 (214), (at [17]–[18]):

> *[T]here are two categories of case in which the court has the power to stay proceedings for abuse of process. These are, first,*

> *where the court concludes that the accused can no longer receive a fair hearing; and, second, where it would otherwise be unfair to try the accused or, put another way, where a stay is necessary to protect the integrity of the criminal justice system.*

In relation to the issues envisaged above, as was confirmed in the case of *Wotton (R on the application of) v Central Devon Magistrates Court* [2003] EWHC 146 (Admin), the magistrates' court is able to stay such proceedings.

Applications are run under the second limb; that it would be unfair for the proceedings against to continue, and therefore a stay is necessary to protect the integrity of the criminal justice system. Moreover an application ought advance that to continue the proceedings in all the circumstances would offend the court's sense of justice and propriety.

DPP v P [2007] EWHC 946 (Admin) provides some guidance for when the court might, finally, resort to abuse of process . Lady Justice Smith considered in that case that that where effective participation is raised as the issue on an abuse of process application, the court would hear medical evidence as part of evidence in the case as part of the trial (rather than on free – standing application). The court, having heard this evidence and having a weather eye to the defendant's participation, would then have a discretion to proceed with a fact-finding hearing (under section 37(3) of the MHA) or to stay the proceedings as an abuse of process.

One key phrase deployed in that case is that the court would reach the point of a stay only if "no useful purpose at all could be served by finding the facts". It is surmised that by this, if it is clear there is literally no prospect of either a guardianship or hospital order, then there would be no useful purpose identifiable; why proceed to find facts upon which no order can be made?

Result of a Stay

Inevitably, if the case is stayed as an abuse, there is no disposal the court can order.

This is problematic in two ways; firstly, the defendant does not receive any help which may well, in an era of scarce provision, have been of great assistance to him.

Vice versa, the prosecution was brought because of concerns that he committed an offence; there was evidence he had done so, and a public interest in trying the issue. Instead there is simply no result. This cannot have been parliament's intent when drafting the respective magistrates' and Crown Court schemes.

Sine Die

There remains one remaining option – the court is able, as a last resort, to attempt to adjourn "sine die". *Henderson v CPS* [2016] EWHC 464 (Admin), [2016] 1 WLR 1990

This would be a deeply unattractive choice for any court and it is unfortunately only available in relation to summary only charges. It is clearly not available for Defendants who face either way offences for the following reasons:

- s.10(4) Magistrates' Court Act 1980 sets out that the accused "shall" be remanded if the offence is triable either way (ie. it's mandatory).

- s10(2) states "The court may when adjourning either fix the time and place at which the trial is to be resumed, or, unless it remands the accused, leave the time and place to be determined later by the court"

- Therefore, if the defendant is remanded (which by virtue of 10(4) he must be), the court cannot leave the time and place to be later determined and so has to fix a date.

Thus, the court cannot adjourn sine die in triable either way matters.

In any event there is, in this author's view, a strong case for this never being the best route for a court to take. The – necessarily vulnerable – defendant would for the foreseeable future have the mater hanging over his head. This cannot be the manner in which it might be best thought to dispose of a case.

Conclusion

For all the reasons above the magistrates' and youth courts are ill equipped to deal with fitness to plead as an issue and the regime requires a complete overhaul. There has been review of this, not least of which in a Law Commission Report (no. 364) which is of great use to any practitioner in the area. As of yet this area has not been rationalised and thus the cats' cradle above rules fitness to plead proceedings in the magistrates' court.

CHAPTER THREE

CROWN COURT

Introduction

By comparison with the magistrates' court, the procedure in the Crown Court in relation to fitness to plead is mercifully clearer.

The act which governs the Crown Court regime is the somewhat antiquely named Criminal Procedure (Insanity) Act 1964.

There are three key sub sections which govern the process:

- s.4: The procedure for determining whether the defendant is "unfit", or as the act terms it "under a disability"

- s.4A: A jury determines whether the defendant "did the act or made the omission charged against him as the offence". The trial of the act or facts.

- s.5: The options the court has in terms of disposal. (Limited to hospital orders, supervision order, or absolute discharge)

The act is, to a degree, outdated and there is increasing debate as to whether it addresses sufficiently how the court should approach those with learning difficulties or other participation issues which do not amount to a "mental disorder" within the meaning of the act.

As ever there will always be a balancing act between protecting the rights of the vulnerable defendant(and even trying to assist with his recovery) weighted against the need to protect the public.

Even within the need to protect vulnerable defendants there is a duality to "what is in their best interests"; the current law can on occasion be something of a sledgehammer to crack a nut, with defendants either being "fit" or "unfit". If deemed unfit their ability to participate in their own trial is curtailed even if they are partially able to give instructions. This does not always make room for any legal agency on a defendant's part.

So too, if a defendant is deemed technically "fit" the court can find itself dealing with someone with quite severe learning difficulties and a need to radically adapt the trial process so that they can participate.

As it stands there is no "sliding scale". A defendant is fit to plead and stand trial, or they are not. It may be this is an area for there to be consideration of reform in the future.

Of proceedings under the act do not involve the determination of a criminal charge within the meaning of article 6 ECHR. There can be no punishment arising from them; only the disposals outlined above. This, in some way places limits on the powers of the courts when there could otherwise be a swinging ability to punish the mentally vulnerable by proving only a trial of the act.

Burden and Standard

Firstly it is of use to discuss who the burden is on to establish fitness to plead.

If the defendant raises it as an issue then he must prove he is unfit on the balance of probabilities.

Vice versa if he contests it as an issue the prosecution raise then it is for the prosecution to satisfy the court beyond a reasonable doubt that he is unfit (*R v Robertson* [1968] 1 WLR 1767).

Section 4 and The Pritchard Test: Establishing the Defendant is Unfit

The framework regarding how the court must proceed is set down in s.4 as outlined above. s.4 reads as follows:

Criminal Procedure (Insanity) Act 1964, s.4

> *(1) This section applies where on the trial of a person the question arises (at the instance of the defence or otherwise) whether the accused is under a disability, that is to say, under any disability such that apart from this Act it would constitute a bar to his being tried.*
>
> *(2) If, having regard to the nature of the supposed disability, the court are of opinion that it is expedient to do so and in the interests of the accused, they may postpone consideration of the question of fitness to be tried until any time up to the opening of the case for the defence.*
>
> *(3) If, before the question of fitness to be tried falls to be determined, the jury return a verdict of acquittal on the count or each of the counts on which the accused is being tried, that question shall not be determined.*
>
> *(4) Subject to subsections (2) and (3) above, the question of fitness to be tried shall be determined as soon as it arises.*
>
> *(5) The question of fitness to be tried shall be determined by the court without a jury.*
>
> *(6) The court shall not make a determination under subsection (5) above except on the written or oral evidence of two or more registered medical practitioners at least one of whom is duly approved.*

Who ought Raise the Issue?

It is of note that the judge, if she is concerned, has a responsibility to raise the issue of fitness to plead. *Erskine; Williams* [2009] EWCA Crim 1425; [2009] 2 Cr. App. R. 29.

Naturally a defendant's representatives will be the first to raise the issue but if, for whatever reason, it is apparent to a judge that a defendant requires assessment, it is incumbent on her to raise it.

Indeed it is made crystal clear in Crim PR 25.10:

> *(1) (…) where—*
>
> *(a) it appears to the court, on application or on its own initiative, that the defendant may not be fit to be tried; and*
>
> *(b) the defendant has not by then been acquitted of each offence charged by the indictment.*
>
> *(2) The court—*
>
> *(a) must exercise its power to decide, without a jury, whether the defendant is fit to be tried*

When must fitness be determined?

As per Crim PR 25.10, this time s.(2) (b), the court may postpone the exercise of that power until immediately before the opening of the defence case if needs be.

it is however more usual that as soon as it is discovered the defendant might be unfit, that this assessment process and determination is undertaken prior to any trial listing. Mental wellbeing is of course not always stable, and many defendants' wellbeing fluctuates, especially should they have been remanded into custody while awaiting trial. The ability of the court not to determine the issue until just before the defence case is called, and therefore the defendant called to give evidence, makes room for this mutability.

Importantly, once the issue is raised it must be determined (*R v Orr* [2016] EWCA Crim 89). If it is clear that a defendant is no longer fit to participate then a judge must follow the s.4A procedure. It cannot be avoided.

"Under a Disability"

The Pritchard test, as reviewed and summarised in the case of *R v M* [2003] EWCA Crim 3452is the test which the court has to follow:

A defendant must be capable of:

- Understanding the charges;
- Deciding whether he wishes to plead guilty;
- Exercising his right to challenge jurors;
- Giving those representing him instructions;
- Following the course of proceedings; AND
- Giving evidence

This test ought be applied in the context of the case which is being tried; matters will be very different regarding a defendant's comprehension when one compares a tax fraud and a pub fight. This ought be kept in mind when the test is applied to the facts. (*Marcantonio; Chitolie* [2016] EWCA Crim 14; [2016] 2 Cr. App. R. 9).

Of note the different parts of this test such as "whether the defendant is capable of understanding the charges" and communicating with his legal advisers are separate; if one part fails, the defendant is not fit to plead.

So too, it ought be noted, even if the court thinks that the defendant is not acting in his own best interest, this is not at all determinative; a court may conclude that a defendant has highly abnormal mental functioning but that does not mean that he does not meet the test above (*Berry* (1978) 66 Cr. App. R. 156, CA).

Amnesia surrounding the events of a crime does not mean the defendant is unfit to plead. Delusions are also not determinative of this. Malingering, ie feigned mental illness, is also looked for by the court.

The reasoning the categories are restrictive is because the disposals are so limited; the court can only order hospital orders, supervision orders and absolute discharge. This limits the court's powers severely, both to help the defendant and protect the community.

Requirement: Two Reports

While a judge can determine that a defendant is *fit* to plead without receiving medical evidence on the point (*R v Ghulam (Habib)* [2009] EWCA Crim 2285, in order to reach a finding he is "unfit" the court must have evidence before it from two "s.12" qualified medical practitioners. (*Lederman* [2015] EWCA Crim 1308; [2016] R.T.R. 16).

As stated in s.4(6) (6) The court shall not make a determination under subsection (5) above except on the written or oral evidence of two or more registered medical practitioners at least one of whom is duly approved.

"Section 12 qualified" is defined by s.8 of the 1964 act *"duly approved* in relation to a registered medical practitioner, means approved for the purposes of s.12 of the Mental Health Act 1983 by the Secretary of State, or by another person by virtue of s.12ZA or 12ZB of that Act, as having "special experience in the diagnosis or treatment of mental disorder".

The Court has the power to remand a defendant to hospital under s.35 or s.36 of the Mental Health Act 1983 for assessment, should he not already have been transferred there by a prison under s.48 (the prison's power to transfer a defendant should they think he needs treatment they cannot provide on a healthcare wing).

With regards to the commissioning of those reports the Criminal Procedure Rules 2020, r.3.10, and Criminal Practice Direction 3P: Commissioning Medical Reports provide guidance as regards the directions the court ought set down.

Special Measures

The defence advocate should always have at the forefront of their mind whether special measures such as video links or intermediaries might allow a defendant to participate in trial "before [taking] the very significant step of embarking on a trial of fitness to plead" *R. v. Walls.* [2011] EWCA Crim 443.

Proceeding under fitness to plead measures is after all a way in which the defendant's legal agency is severely curtailed; if there is any way of proceeding to trial without resorting to it, this ought be encouraged.

Any s.12 qualified psychiatrist assessing a defendant ought be alive to the availability of special measures such as intermediaries to try to address difficulties which might otherwise render a defendant unfit.

A court will, in line with *Walls*, "rigorously examine" any reports before proceeding to find that the defendant is unfit. Even if both s.12 experts agree the court is not bound by their findings and must apply their evidence to the statutory scheme.

So too, if a defendant 'becomes fit' again after a s.4 procedure has occurred, another s.4 hearing is needed so as to avoid the need to go down the actus reus trial route – *R. (Hasani) v Crown Court at Blackfriars* [2005] EWHC 3016 (Admin).

If unfit, must appoint advocate

The court must consider carefully who is the best person to be appointed to put the case for the defence (s 4A(2) (b)).

This is repeated in Crim PR 25.10 (3 – "where the court determines that the defendant is not fit to be tried (a) the court must exercise its power to appoint a person to put the case for the defence"; it is a mandatory requirement for the court to check the advocate is competent to dela with the issues raised.

It is hard to see how, in reality, this would be dealt with by a court unless there was clear evidence of incompetence; it is perhaps better thought of as a power the court has to ensure that an unrepresented defendant is able to secure representation.

Actus Reus Trial

s.4A relates to "finding that the accused did the act or made the omission charged against him". It reads as follows:

> *(1) This section applies where in accordance with section 4(5) above it is determined by a court that the accused is under a disability.*
>
> *(2) The trial shall not proceed or further proceed but it shall be determined by a jury—*
>
> > *(a) on the evidence (if any) already given in the trial; and*
> >
> > *(b) on such evidence as may be adduced or further adduced by the prosecution, or adduced by a person appointed by the court under this section to put the case for the defence,*
>
> *whether they are satisfied, as respects the count or each of the counts on which the accused was to be or was being tried, that he did the act or made the omission charged against him as the offence.*
>
> *(3) If as respects that count or any of those counts the jury are satisfied as mentioned in subsection (2) above, they shall make a finding that the accused did the act or made the omission charged against him.*
>
> *(4) If as respects that count or any of those counts the jury are not so satisfied, they shall return a verdict of acquittal as if on the count in question the trial had proceeded to a conclusion.*
>
> *(5) Where the question of disability was determined after arraignment of the accused, the determination under*

> *subsection (2) is to be made by the jury by whom he was being tried.*

As can be seen from the subsection, unlike the issue of fitness itself which is determined by a judge alone, this must be tried by a jury.

That jury must only be sure that the defendant "that did the act or made the omission charged against him as the offence.". There is therefore, nominally, no consideration of mens rea in this exercise what 'went on' in the defendant's mind is essentially put aside, the logic being he is unable to instruct what it was that was going on in his mind.

Of note, his mental state at the time may well also afford a defendant a defence – this book will go on to discuss the defence of insanity and touch upon other ways a defendant's mental state comes in to play. However, if for example a person is accused of murder but is unfit, then the defence are unable to raise diminished responsibility as an issue within an actus reus hearing.

The only distinction, on this issue, is with cases in which a defence is raised on 'objective' evidence; ie evidence of self-defence, accident or mistake. If this is so, the just must be sure beyond reasonable doubt that the prosecution have negatived such a case to the criminal standard. (Antoine [2001] 1 A.C. 340, HL) The defence cannot raise this, however, in the absence of any evidence indicating as much. A jury will inevitably need to decide this issue based on the evidence of witnesses in the crown's case alone ie bystanders to a fight or a car crash. They will need to infer, when considering the evidence, whether accident or self-defence operate on the facts, in absence of the defendant's contribution as it is almost certain a defendant would not be giving evidence in these circumstances.

Each case must be carefully considered, and the offence and facts must be weighed together to determine which elements, precisely, need to be proven. For example in voyeurism, there need to be deliberate observation and a purpose of sexual gratification. Both elements must be established within an actus reus trial; however, 'reasonable belief in consent' is not relevant in such proceedings. s: B (M) [2012] EWCA Crim 770.

Some complexity arises with joint enterprise and primary and secondary participation. Again, case dependent, it may be the jury need to assess (on the objective evidence) whether the Crown can prove that a defendant joined the enterprise or assisted the principle, for example. As above, every case will turn on the combination of facts and charge.

Evidence to be Called in Trial of the Fact

An actus reus trial constitutes "criminal proceedings" with respect to rules of evidence. Hearsay and bad character provisions remain as per a Crown Court trial. See *Chal* [2007] EWCA Crim 2647 and *Creed* [2010] EWCA Crim 2578.

There is no reason, if it seems clear that the defendant was well at the time of it, that the interview cannot be relied upon in principle. However, caution may be needed if prosecutors are to rely on it that it does not muddy the waters (given the inability to look into mens rea).

Moreover it is likely s.78 arguments to exclude the interview, especially if made in the face of the weight of psychiatric evidence obtained since, may succeed as a court will likely seek reassurance that there was certainly no issue with the defendant being unfit at the time. If it is admitted the direction given to the jury must be very particularly tailored to the facts of the case and the elements the Crown must prove or disprove given the risk he may have said something as a result of the 'disability' the Court must have found he was operating under.

In light of the above general propositions, what evidence, then, needs to be called in the finding of the fact? This is always a difficult question. Can a defence advocate agree any evidence if their client is entirely unable to give instructions? Different advocates take different approaches on this issue; some take the view that if the case is such that nothing would usually be contested, the whole case might be read s.9. Others take the view that if they have no instructions, they can agree nothing, and all witnesses must be warned to attend court.

Without deprecating the latter course unduly, unless there is on the face of the papers material upon which witnesses ought be cross-examined, it is not envisaged that an actus reus trial will often require the attendance of *all* witnesses in a case; an example where it may be required is if defending counsel has strong suspicions that all police officers in a case have provided misleading statements upon which all need to be cross-examined. This is rarely the case but defence should obviously not be barred from ensuring such evidence is rigorously scrutinised, even more so when their client is incapacitated.

However, other cases might only require the attendance of only the complainant, say in an allegation of rape or assault in which there are clear points of inconsistency or self-defence to put. In yet other cases the incident may be caught on CCTV and therefore the nature of the evidence is rather more the focus of interpretation in a speech to the jury at the close of the case. Each case, therefore, will require a specific assessment, therefore, of whether evidence is to be called live, and if so, which witnesses in light of the elements to be proven or disproven on the specific facts.

Disposals

As noted above, the court is limited in disposals given the defendant's 'disability. Once the act is found under s.4A, the Court is limited to the disposals in s.5 which are designed to help the defendant with treatment and support. At most the disposals have a restrictive element so that the community might be protected (ie s.37 hospital orders and s.41 hospital orders with restriction).

The orders available under s.5 are:

- Hospital orders under s.37 or s.41 (with or without restriction)
- Supervision orders
- Absolute discharge

Again, there is debate as to whether these are sufficient for current purposes, there being limited resources for supervision orders in the community in particular. Similarly, they make no room for a defendant who may benefit from the slightly 'looser' nature of a mental health treatment requirement as attached to a suspended sentence, if indeed he is much better due to medication being provided and adhered to, for example.

Of note these are the same disposals available to the court when the defendant is found to have been "not guilty due to insanity", the alternative verdict outside of "guilty" or "not guilty" that a jury are entitled to come to when that defence has been run (more on which later).

Hospital Orders

Hospital orders are governed by s.37 MHA:

> *(1) Where a person is convicted before the Crown Court of an offence punishable with imprisonment other than an offence the sentence for which is fixed by law, or is convicted by a magistrates' court of an offence punishable on summary conviction with imprisonment, and the conditions mentioned in subsection (2) below are satisfied, the court may by order authorise his admission to and detention in such hospital as may be specified in the order or, as the case may be, place him under the guardianship of a local social services authority or of such other person approved by a local social services authority as may be so specified. (…)*
>
> *(2) The conditions referred to in subsection (1) above are that —*
>
> *(a) the court is satisfied, on the written or oral evidence of two registered medical practitioners, that the offender is suffering from mental disorder and that either—*
>
> *(i) the mental disorder from which the offender is suffering is of a nature or degree which makes it appropriate for him to be detained in a hospital for medical treatment and appropriate medical treatment is available for him; or*
>
> *(ii) in the case of an offender who has attained the age of 16 years, the mental disorder is of a nature or degree which warrants his reception into guardianship under this Act; and*

(b) the court is of the opinion, having regard to all the circumstances including the nature of the offence and the character and antecedents of the offender, and to the other available methods of dealing with him, that the most suitable method of disposing of the case is by means of an order under this section.

The conditions which must be satisfied are outlined in the statute above.

They initially last for six months, can be extended for another six and then again at yearly intervals where the responsible medical officer considers further detention necessary for the protection of the public or in the interests of the patient's health or safety.

At least one of the two medical practitioners referred to in s. 37(2) must be approved, for the purposes of s. 12, by the Secretary of State, as having special experience in the diagnosis or treatment of mental disorder.

It would appear, in contrast to guardianship orders, that the lower limit for a hospital order is 10, there being no definition of a lower age for hospital orders within the act (for guardianship orders the lower limit is 16).

The purposes of a hospital order are rehabilitation of the patient and protection of the public; it is not concerned with punishment (*Fisher* [2019] EWCA Crim 1066).

The court must be assured that there is a bed available – this is a requirement written into statute within s.37(4)

A court is able to make an interim hospital order whilst establishing whether the full order is required. The qualifying conditions under s.38 are virtually the same as for the making of a hospital order under

s. 37, however one of the expert witnesses must work at the hospital where the defendant is to be detained. This order only lasts for 12 weeks, renewable for periods of 28 days.

It is of note that the court remains empowered to order a hospital order with restriction under s.41 in relation to an actus reus trial. Effectively where the court, having regard to the nature of the offence the defendant's antecedents and the risk of further offences, consider it necessary for the protection of the public from serious harm so to do, the court can order the defendant to be subject of special restrictions. Those restrictions are set out in s.41(3).

The court can take its own view as to whether it accepts medical evidence on this point before it.

Unlike an order under s.37 a s.41 order does not lapse but continues as long as the order remains in place. Discharge occurs only when the patient satisfies the First-tier Tribunal that he poses no unacceptable risk to the public.

Supervision Orders

Supervision orders, governed by the Criminal Procedure (Insanity) Act 1964 s.5 entail supervision of the defendant by the local authority or a probation worker.

Such orders can include a residence requirement or a treatment requirement.

Before the court can make a supervision order it must have evidence supervision is available and arranged (*City and County of Swansea v Swansea Crown Court* [2016] EWHC 1389 (Admin).

Indeed, the relevant officer must consent to the making of the order, and be named in the making of the order.

There is no method of reviewing this order or monitoring or taking action on any breach of it.

It is therefore the least favoured order; the court cannot take action in the result of breach and there are vanishingly scarce resources to allow for its creation in the first place.

Absolute Discharge

This may be the only realistic option left to the court if medical evidence reveals a defendant is essentially 'well' again. As per the supervision order there is limited power afforded to the court in the event of another incident occurring. It is however an essential tool in the court's arsenal given the lack of blame of many caught up in mental health crisis events, and thus within the criminal justice system.

Other Orders

Real consideration is needed when considering other orders available to the court. For example it may be that the prosecution seek a Sexual Harm Prevention Order, or Violent Offender Order. However, defence may well need to be alive to the fact that their client has limited functioning and understanding to cope with such orders, or indeed understand them in the first place.

Abuse of Process

When considering a defendant's ability to participate in criminal proceedings the abuse of process jurisprudence should also be considered. There is a segment on the same in the magistrates' court section of this book, it being a measure used when the inadequate procedures in that court do not meet the needs of the situation.

Where a defendant lacks the ability through (for example) age, lack of maturity, social functioning, intellect emotional and mental capacity proceedings may be stayed as an abuse of process (see, *T and V v. United Kingdom* (2000) 31 EHRR 861, *SC v. United Kingdom* (2005) 40 EHRR 10, *Subramaniam v. the Queen* [2004] HCA 51 and *R (TP) v. West London Youth Court* [2005] EWHC 2583(Admin)).

Appealing an unfitness / actus reus

There are a number of appeals of actus reus hearing findings and there are a disproportionately higher number of appeals against determinations under ss.4 and 4A than 'normal' trials. While no detail is gone into here, it is key that the advocate dealing with the case remains alive to any aspect of proceedings which might engender an appeal.

Normal rules of evidence apply and given the 'case specific' nature of the directions for the actus reus hearing it may well be there is thought to be given to whether fairness was achieved.

In *R. v Roberts (Alfred)* the court considered whether a defendant representing himself (who was adjudged not fit) was able to lodge grounds of appeal. ([2019] EWCA Crim 1270). Essentially the view was that it falls to the appointed person (the defence representative) to advise on appeal.

While, if they think they are able, the defence representative may have regard to what instructions can be gleaned from the defendant, they are clearly not beholden to them given they arise from someone adjudged unfit to plead or instruct.

CHAPTER FOUR

INSANITY

This next chapter relates to the so called "special verdict" of insanity.

It is essential to make reference to this third option of "not guilty by reason of insanity" which is open to juries as it is important that the distinction between fitness to plead procedures and defences are clear. There are after all a number of ways in which mental health is central to the consideration of how someone is dealt with in the criminal justice system. Defences to the offence, ways that the court ought manage the trial process and trial, and disposals which involve treatment and the protection of the public rather than punishment are different categories.

The courts have developed fitness to plead procedures to cope with the management of a mentally vulnerable defendant who cannot withstand the trial process. Naturally this is someone who is unwell during the court process. That person may have been "well" at the time of the offence. They may not. Either way, there is a division between the statutes and case law managing the process ("fitness to plead" provisions) and the defences which someone might avail themselves relating to the crime which is alleged.

In one sense a bare assertion that he 'lacks mens rea' may be one defence run.

Another may be non-insane/"sane" automatism. Briefly, automatism relates to "the complete destruction of voluntary control"; ie none of the defendant's conduct was voluntary – the defence need to produce an evidential foundation to show that (for reasons unconnected with a 'disease of the mind') the defendant's control was completely destroyed.

In cases of murder "diminished responsibility" or "loss of control" may arise as a partial defence to the charge in question.

So too, intoxication, while not a 'defence' per se, will also possibly play into whether or not a defendant can form the mens rea required although it should be noted that the courts are quick in most cases to "shut down" any avenue upon which a defendant might seek to rely on a reliance on drink or drugs to "get away" with an offence.

All of the above are noted in passing. They are relevant as the intersection of mental health defences and lack of mens rea is where insanity also falls. The former are "complete" defences which would result in acquittal.

When, however, someone suffers from a "defect of reason" brought about by a "disease of the mind" the insanity provisions are available for the defendant and if the verdict is reached by the jury, allow for specific disposals which treat the defendant.

Lord Denning provided a renowned example which is oft used to explain the intersection between defences in this rea of a man throwing something onto a fire. He thought it was a log. It was in fact a baby. While he might have availed himself of defences such as automatism or lack of mens rea, as will be seen below it is very much the sort of case in which the verdict of insanity is likely to come into play due to the man either "not knowing nature and quality of the act" he was undertaking, or not knowing it was wrong.

A jury can return an entirely separate verdict to that available to them in the usual course of a trial. Instead of reliance on "guilty" and "not guilty" as a resolution to a trial, they can instead return a verdict of "insanity".

The "Special Verdict"

The 'special verdict' of 'not guilty by reason of insanity' is provided for in the Trial of Lunatics Act 1883, s. 2:

> *"Where in any indictment or information any act or omission is charged against any person as an offence, and it is given in evidence on the trial of such person for that offence that he was insane, so as not to be responsible, according to law, for his action at the time when the act was done or omission made, then, if it appears to the jury before whom such person is tried that he did the act or made the omission charged, but was insane as aforesaid at the time when he did or made the same, the jury shall return a special verdict that the accused is not guilty by reason of insanity."*

It is important to note that this is a verdict which must be returned by a jury, and cannot be a "plea" from the defendant, even if both defence and prosecution entirely agree on all psychiatric evidence – R. v. Crown Court at Maidstone, ex p. London Borough of Harrow [2000] 1 Cr.App.R. 117, DC

This may result in a tribunal's incredulity that the case cannot be resolved with a plea; the situation is however clear that the jury must consider the material and make their own determination as to whether such a verdict can be returned after a trial of the act.

It will remain open to them, however perverse it might seem on the medical evidence, to return a verdcit of guilt. Vice versa they are also able to acquit if they consider the evidence proving the 'act' not to meet the criminal standard.

As can be inferred above, a trial of the act must still take place. The trial of the act takes the same form as that described in the "fitness to plead" chapter, with broadly only the actus reus being proven (although with some added fault elements sometimes incorporated, and as per the case of Antoine, with some defences considered if raised on objective evidence).

The Test

The law in this area is of some antiquity, as is indicated by the word "insane" used at its heart (long fallen out of favour in psychiatric practice).

The case at its heart is M'Naghten's Case (1843) 10 Cl & F 200. Within that case the essentials were set out which have remained central to the establishment of the special verdict;

> (…) the jurors ought to be told in all cases that *every man is to be presumed to be sane,* and to possess a sufficient degree of reason to be responsible for his crimes, *until the contrary be proved to their satisfaction;* and that to establish a defence on the ground of insanity, it must be clearly proved that, *at the time of the committing of the act,* the party accused was labouring under such *a defect of reason, from disease of the mind, as not to know the nature and quality of the act he was doing; or,* if he did know it, *that he did not know he was doing what was wrong.*

This paragraph has formed into the "M'Naghten Rules", and each phrase must be looked into in a discussion of this area of the law.

Of note it is the legal test which prevails, not medical opinion irrespective of how unwell a defendant may seem.

"Until the contrary be proved otherwise"

Firstly, the burden is contained within this paragraph. When the prosecution bring the case and remain under the criminal burden of proving the 'act' to the jury so that they are "sure", the defence when raising insanity must only prove it to the balance of probabilities; this is "until the contrary be proved otherwise".

The logic is of course that in proving insanity a defendant may well be, to a degree, disadvantaged as he will possibly be prevented from running defences such as sane automatism. In addition until relatively recently there were very few disposals available which made running insanity deeply unattractive.

Thus, the defence must prove the defendant is not sane but only to the lower standard.

"At the time of committing the act"

This provision notes, as per the distinction above, that insanity is concerned with the defendant's mental state at the time of the offence. "Fitness to plead" provisions are distinct to this and dealt with in the entirely separate procedures discussed elsewhere in this book.

"Defect" of reason

The key issue with regards to a "defect of reason" is that the defendant has departed from any sense of rationality. It was discussed in the case of Clarke [1972] 1 All ER 219. The Court of Appeal held in that case that an absent-minded failure to actually use his powers of reasoning were not sufficient for this to be mounted (albeit they could amount to a defence of lack of mens rea).

There is a key distinction within this between those operating under "insane automatism" ie they operate in a completely involuntary way as a result of a "disease of the mind" and sane automatism. The latter would attract an acquittal as a full defence; the former would attract the insanity verdict. Extremely thorough psychiatric evidence would be required, for example, at the intersection of diabetes and insulin loss of consciousness with reported mental ill health in the background due to the concerning level of overlap with regards to whether a defence might be run, or insanity provisions utilised.

"Disease of the Mind"

Whether or not a defendant was suffering from a disease of the mind' is a legal question for the judge to decide rather than a medical one. Essentially the cause of the defendant's "mental defect" is the issue, and indeed that the defendant's mental faculties were impaired. From those two aspects of the evidence the judge can determine the issue as to whether he was suffering from a disease of the mind.

As per the fitness to plead provisions the evidence of at least two registered medical practitioners is required, this time by s1 of the Criminal Procedure (Insanity and Unfitness to Plead) Act 1991.

As noted above, external factors such as ingestion of drink or drugs ought not be kept in mind when considering this defence. They would lift the case away from one in which the "defect of reason" was one at which the root was a "disease of the mind".

So too taking an anaesthetic or possibly taking insulin may mean that there are other factors which lift the case out of those classed as subject to insanity provisions.

In cases of sleepwalking again an intersection between automatism and insanity might be found; in the case of Burgess [1991] 2 QB 92 it was found to be 'internal' and therefore subject to insanity. The overlap is however clear and will always be a matter for anxious consideration by an advocate on available medical evidence.

"Did not know the nature and quality of the act" and "Did not know that what he was doing was wrong"

Not knowing the nature and quality of the act was effectively summarised by Diplock LJ in the case of Sullivan [1984] in which he re-stated it as the defendant "did not know what he was doing".

It refers to the physical nature of "doing the act". An example as already referred to above would be the man Lord Denning referred to unaware he was throwing a baby on a fire, not a log.

With regards to whether or not the defendant "knew what he was doing was wrong" there has been much debate over whether the issue was whether he knew what he did was "legally" or "morally" wrong.

After some consternation by the courts the concept that ' "wrong" means "contrary to law" was applied in *Johnson* [2007] EWCA Crim 1978 and again in *Keal* [2022] EWCA Crim 341. The court in that case summarised the position: "In our judgment, 'wrong' means both against the law and wrong by the standards of ordinary reasonable people. Strictly a jury must be satisfied that the defendant did not know that what he was doing was against the law nor wrong by the standards of reasonable ordinary people. In practice how the jury is directed on this issue will depend on the facts and issues in the particular case."

In Keal the court had in fact accepted that in essence there would be a wide definition of defect of reason, but in turn the verdict would require a defendant lacks both legal and moral wrongness knowledge.

Insanity can operate in relation to a strict liability offence or an offence with an objective element, if the person comes to be doing what is criminal because of a delusion as to its nature and quality: *Loake v DPP* [2017] EWHC 2855 (Admin).

Disposals

The orders available to the court mirror those available for fitness to plead and are not repeated here. They remain the only options available to the court, no matter the gravity of the offence.

Therefore the court can make a hospital order, with or without restriction; a supervision order, with or without a treatment requirement or give an absolute discharge.

Magistrates

The defence of insanity is available in the magistrates' courts. If there is a finding made, the result is a complete acquittal as per *Horseferry Road Magistrates' Court, ex parte K*[1997] QB 23 and *R (Singh) v Stratford Magistrates' Court* [2007] EWHC 1582 (Admin). That being said it is rarely used in this jurisdiction and it is likely to remain so.

The need for robust medical evidence confirming it as a truly viable defence would no doubt be thoroughly examined by magistrates.

CHAPTER FIVE

AUTOMATISM

It is of use addressing the defence of automatism at this stage given it is so closely interwoven with the issues which arise in insanity cases, as briefly mentioned above.

The Law Commission, when considering reform, has found that automatism and insanity are so closely interrelated that "reform of one entails reform of the other".

In Bratty versus Attorney General for Northern Ireland, 1963 (1AC, 386), Lord Denning defined this defence. Automatism is:

> *"(...) an act which is done by the muscles without any control by the mind such as a spasm, a reflex action or a convulsion; or an act done by a person who is not conscious of what he is doing such as an act done while suffering from concussion or while sleepwalking"*

Sometimes called "non-insane automatism", it is a defence for a defendant to prove that he suffered from a "total destruction of voluntary control" over his actions at the time of the offence Classically as outlined above automatism has effectively involved those suffering from spasms, reflexes, convulsions, although it is not limited to such experiences.

This is a common law defence available for all crimes including those of strict liability.

In another key case in the area R. v Coley (2013) (EWCA 223), the Court defined it as "the essence of it is that the movements or actions of the defendant at the material time were wholly involuntary. The better expression is complete destruction of voluntary control (…) Involuntary' is not the same as 'irrational'; indeed it needs to be sharply distinguished from it."

Examples of automatism can be said to include those who suffer hyper or hypoglycaemic incidents as part of their diabetes, or possibly those who suffer from sleepwalking. Someone suffering an epileptic fit or a stroke may also benefit from the defence.

The most famed example – part of a driving case as so many of the automatism cases are – is that of being stung by a swarm of bees, as discussed in the case of Hill v Baxter [1958]; the defendant stung by a swarm of bees and thus veering off the road has no control over his actions, and that control would certainly be totally destroyed.

In line with other areas of law, especially the law concerning voluntary intoxication, it is no defence if the defendant recklessly imbibed alcohol and/or took drugs.

However, there is a complex inter-relationship when it comes to whether a "disease of the mind" is also in operation and therefore insanity applies, or there was just a destruction of voluntary control, in which case automatism arises, or both apply and the jury must be thus directed.

It is clear and established law that a judge must assess, when determining whether the defence of automatism can be left to the jury:

1. Whether a proper evidential foundation has been established by the defence; and

2. Whether the case falls within the M'Nagten rules or non-insane automatism.

Thus, importantly, it is for the defence to raise the issue of automatism. The defence must then produce evidence to discharge their evidential burden – a "proper evidential foundation". The case of C [2007] EWCA Crim 1862 was an example of a defendant essentially having to be called to give evidence so the defence had discharged the burden.

This, it would seem is the only real way to properly establish in evidence that all control had in fact been destroyed if extraneous evidence points only to impairment, irrationality or disinhibition. None of these are sufficient to amount to the "total loss" of control the law requires for this defence to be effective.

If the defence discharge that evidential burden it then falls to the Crown to negative automatism to the criminal standard. The prosecution will in such circumstances usually seek to demonstrate that either the evidence demonstrates he was entirely conscious at the time, or that he was 'reckless' with regards to how the "total destruction of voluntary control" came about.

It is of note that if insanity and automatism are live in the same case there are distinct burdens – it is for the defence to prove insanity 'on the balance'; it is for the Crown to disprove automatism to the criminal standard.

Much of the case law has focussed on this intersection.

The case of Quick [1978] QB 918 is a foundational case in the area.

Of note, the case assisted with determining why hypoglycaemia fell under automatism and not insanity – essentially the issue was that the "malfunction of the mind" of "transitory effect" was caused by the "application to the body of some external factor". Those factors might include violence, drugs, anaesthesia, alcohol or hypnosis. An involuntary state induced by any of those could be, by operation of the external factor, be said to be a disease of the mind.

The principle that automatism can never be a defence for someone if they had "reasonably foreseen" the incapacity coming about was therefore gone into in some detail.

Examples of times when someone might "reasonably foresee" the incapacity would be drinking while on a prescription drug which clearly contra-indicated alcohol. Similarly the issue of eating without appropriate insulin intake (if a diagnosed diabetic) might be thought to have some foreseeable results.

In the case of Quick, a diabetic, important questions that arose included when the defendant last ate, whether he knew he was going into a 'hypo', and why or whether he did not try to resolve the issue by eating a sugar cube as he had been told to do. One might also ask why he did not pull over his car at the first sign of a hypo, it probably having to have gone quite some way for him to have lapsed out of consciousness. Each case will turn on its own facts but this gives an idea of the nature of the questions the defence will have to grapple with when considering advancing a case of automatism.

Vice versa the case of Burns [1974] 58 Cr App R 364 CA it was found that a judge should leave both insanity and automatism to the jury. The circumstances of that case were that of someone with a severe alcohol addiction who suffered periods of amnesia caused by brain damage. On the day the defendant had taken both a prescribed drug and alcohol. As there was a clear "external factor" here (the drug and the alcohol) the defence of automatism had to be left to the jury alongside insanity; it was for the Crown to prove that taking that drug and alcohol were reckless in the circumstances.

The case of Bailey [1983] 2 All ER 503 followed. This case reaffirmed the principle that if the defendant knew he was taking a course which might well lead to his being in an uncontrollable state, and he took no action to remedy or prevent that, then automatism is not available to him.

The case of Bailey however raised the perennial issue of the intersection of voluntary intoxication and automatism. The case noted that in a s.18 grievous bodily harm case self-induced intoxication would still be an available defence as the offence is one of strict liability.

One clear example of a case which did not reach the required level of "complete destruction" of control was that discussed in AG Ref (2 of 1992) (1993) 97 Cr App R 429. In that case a lorry driver crashed. He advanced evidence (an expert) who stated he was suffering from a condition "driving without awareness" in which while he would have had some knowledge of what was going on, the repetitive stimuli of long-distance driving lulls one into a 'haze' of sorts. The court firmly rejected this as an example of "total" destruction of control, noting clearly that "impaired" or "reduced" control was simply insufficient.

Sleepwalking was considered in the case of Burgess (1991) 93 Cr App R 41 CA. In that case the defendant wounded his victim by hitting her while sleepwalking with an object. The disorder appeared, in that case, due to an "internal factor". The court was concerned as to the risk that it was the sort of "internal" factor that might reoccur and manifest in violence. For those reasons the court determined in that case the right operation of law would be for the court to determine the sleepwalking a "disease of the mind", and thus determine that insanity operated.

Vice versa, in Roach [2001] EWCA Crim 2698 the defendant had mixed personality disorder and he had taken prescription drugs and drank alcohol. Here it was ruled automatism ought to have been left to the jury following the rules in Quick that some form of "external" factor had impacted on the defendant's state of mind. Again however one might as a defence advocate need to consider the ramifications of the "reasonableness" test – that the defendant needed to have been acting reasonably in the circumstances.

The issue which one might follow through from the collated case law above is that there will be no "disease of the mind" (ie insanity) where the incapacity was "caused by the application to the body of some external factor such as violence, drugs, including anaesthetics, alcohol and hypnotic influences".

However, this leads to illogical and strange results as demonstrated with the cases relating to diabetes outlined above: in both those cases the relevant mental states may be caused by "external factors" (alcohol or insulin) or "internal factors" (lack of food or insufficient insulin). To quote the Law Commission Discussion Paper on Insanity and Automatism (2013) on the issue, if one assesses the respective cases of diabetics:

> *"The upshot is that a diabetic who, without fault, fails to take insulin and then commits an allegedly criminal act would be treated as insane. In contrast, a diabetic who took insulin in accordance with a medical prescription would be acquitted if they were an automaton at the time of committing an allegedly criminal act."*

So too there are issues that a defendant who retains a degree of capacity may not be able to avail themselves of automatism but might be able to avail themselves of insanity provisions. This seems somewhat about face.

It is also unclear when a defendant suffers a "psychological blow" case in which a defendant apparently enters a dissociative state, perhaps interlinked with PTSD. It remains unclear (due to divergent case law) whether a defendant might avail themselves of insanity or automatism in such a situation. The external and internal issues with automatism as a defence make it hard for courts to place where the impact of another's actions on the dissociation fall; was it a disease of the mind or was an external factor operating?

So too with sleepwalking, sometimes there is an external trigger. Ought this lift sleepwalking out of automatism entirely into the realms of only automatism?

The divide between internal and external triggers seems arbitrary and leads to confusing case law.

From the law as it stands, however, are some principles can be derived which assist those considering whether the defence operates:

- Medical evidence is clearly needed to establish whether a disease of the mind is operating;
- If it is not, or there is also another factor operating, it is possible that automatism applies;
- Was the loss of control "total" (rather than impaired or reduced);
- Was the defendant at fault – a recklessness test is effectively imported into the case law. If a very mentally unwell man takes ketamine knowing the potential effect it might have on him, it is unlikely that the defence will be available to him due to the recklessness that clearly demonstrates;

- Is medical evidence needed to assist the defence case with regards to demonstrating the lack of recklessness ie that a diabetic had acted appropriately and mitigated risk as much as she could, notwithstanding her ultimate total destruction of control.

In simple terms involuntary conduct caused by an "internal factor" is classed as insanity and that leads to the special verdict. Involuntary conduct caused by an "external factor" is classed as (sane) automatism, leading to a simple acquittal.

However, automatism, sitting as it does at the junction of insanity and voluntary intoxication has a number of layers of complexity much as the other defences and legislation in the area.

Running a case on this basis is always a complex exercise and requires consideration of the need of expert evidence at the earliest stages in order to ensure the correct defence is in fact being run.

CHAPTER SIX

CONCLUSION – REFORM AND THE FUTURE

Both fitness to plead and insanity arise out of Victorian legislation. The language is antiquated. The concepts have not kept up either with modern psychiatry or even modern lawyers' appreciation of vulnerability as opposed to any 'moral' of 'character' connotation to "disorders of the mind".

In 2010 the Law Commission proposed provisional ideas on reform to fitness to plead. In 2013 the Law Commission then proposed extensive reform to both automatism and insanity. In 2016 the Law Commission solidified their proposals on Fitness to Plead (after a lengthy process).

Those reforms have not been implemented wholesale, and those 'corners' which have (such as moves towards specialist training for advocates dealing with children and youths) have been relatively small scale.

The issue of fitness to plead was adjudged to be the more urgently in need of reform by the law commission.

The low number of insanity cases was noted and potentially this factored into the reasons why reform on insanity was placed lower in import than fitness to plead, albeit the importance of the 'filtering' nature of fitness to plead proceedings was noted given this procedure lifts out many defendants from the final trial process, preventing the need for a reliance on insanity.

One point to note however is that this was based on 2012 research. It is queried if the numbers of insanity cases are quite so low now in 2023. From anecdotal reports and the crisis in funding with regards to mental health care in the UK this author wonders if there are in fact many more defendants who might fall under this head than are currently being dealt with under it.

One thing that was clear throughout in the feedback to the respective reports was that respondents considered reform to fitness to plead measures the more pressing issue out of the two areas of possible reform, with concerns as to the technical operation of insanity and automatism defences taking a back seat.

As ever the focus is on "outcome" for their clients for those on the ground, so the practitioners feeding back appeared to acknowledge the slightly torturous nature of the interrelated defences but focused more on achieving best outcomes for those within the system.

Thus the Law Commission focused its sights on reform of fitness to plead, acknowledging as it did so that the current tests do not cover the "right abilities" and on occasion the current law sets the test too high. In particular the lack of provision for those with learning difficulties is remarked upon.

The Commission noted the deficiencies of the magistrates' court procedures with some alarm.

They noted their fundamental concerns that people are "being tried when they should not be because of their mental state".

Their recommendations with regards fitness to plead included widening the test to include participation issues and ensuring that the test is uniform across the youth, magistrates' and Crown courts. The test would focus on whether the defendant is able to participate effectively in their trial.

Crucially the authors also acknowledged in their report "if the legal test for unfitness to plead were reformed, then there would probably be an increase in the number of people with serious mental disorder who are found unfit to stand trial".

It is perhaps understandable therefore that this has very firmly been placed on the back burner by Government.

In the Report on the Implementation of Law Commission Recommendations dated July 2023 the following is stated in terms:

> *"… [The Commission provided] their final report and draft Bill [regarding fitness to plead] in January 2016. The Government provided an interim response on 22 February 2016, acknowledging the Commission's work and noting that a substantive response would be provided later. The Government is considering the report's recommendations and will respond to these in due course."*

Glacial perhaps doesn't even cover the progress of this issue given research began in 2010, the report was provided in 2016 and seven years later the Government has stated it will "respond in due course".

Given the urgency in tone of the Law Commission's report on fitness to plead it is of real concern that so little has occurred with regards to reform of the black letter law of this area.

Other jurisdictions have recently updated their legislation in relation to the insanity test; Scotland reformed in 2010 and Ireland in 2006. Australia and Canada reformed by way of case law in recent years. It is well beyond time that England and Wales catch up given the clear recommendations made by the Law Commission over seven years ago.

These issues with reform are compounded by the crisis of funding within mental health care. There is insufficient resource to meet the needs of the criminal justice system in any event, let alone the needs of the mentally vulnerable who so often find themselves within it, both as witnesses and defendants.

Those working within the justice system are clear that the lack of funding has led to ever increasing numbers of defendants being incarcerated as a result of their conditions getting out of hand, their lack of housing, their lack of medication, or their lack of support so that they ar able to remedy any and all of the above.

This lack of funding and increase in the mentally disordered ending up within the criminal justice system is all the more worrying in the face of the continuing existence of criminal procedures which are Victorian in origin and which have been reviewed and determined to require wholesale reform.

In particular the current system egregiously fails those youths who have real issues with effective participation. This, above all, ought be an area of immediate reform. The law does not have the right test in place to determine whether any defendant is well enough to stand trial. The fact that this is known and clearly stated in a Law Commission report, and that the remedy to this outlined seven years ago, is all the more stark when it is considered that there is in fact no statutory test at all in place in the youth court. The need for reform is urgent to prevent ongoing and serious injustice to the youngest and most vulnerable.

The provisions dealing with mental health conditions and learning disorders within the justice system are complex and naturally, to a degree they do need to be flexible. However, as noted there are central issues with the structure of the system at present which – quite aside from antiquated language – result in disparity of outcome when defendants have similar difficulties.

It is hoped this book at least provides an initial road map into how an advocate can best assist those who face charges while mentally vulnerable and understand the framework of the system more generally.

MORE BOOKS BY LAW BRIEF PUBLISHING

A selection of our other titles available now:-

'A Practical Guide to Estate Administration and Crypto Assets' by Richard Marshall
'A Practical Guide to Managing GDPR Data Subject Access Requests – Second Edition' by Patrick O'Kane
'A Practical Guide to Parental Alienation in Private and Public Law Children Cases' by Sam King QC & Frankie Shama
'Contested Heritage – Removing Art from Land and Historic Buildings' by Richard Harwood QC, Catherine Dobson, David Sawtell
'The Limits of Separate Legal Personality: When Those Running a Company Can Be Held Personally Liable for Losses Caused to Third Parties Outside of the Company' by Dr Mike Wilkinson
'A Practical Guide to Transgender Law' by Robin Moira White & Nicola Newbegin
'A Practical Guide to 'Stranded Spouses' in Family Law' by Mani Singh Basi
'A Practical Guide to Residential Freehold Conveyancing' by Lorraine Richardson
'A Practical Guide to Pensions on Divorce for Lawyers' by Bryan Scant
'A Practical Guide to Challenging Sham Marriage Allegations in Immigration Law' by Priya Solanki
'A Practical Guide to Legal Rights in Scotland' by Sarah-Jane Macdonald
'A Practical Guide to New Build Conveyancing' by Paul Sams & Rebecca East
'A Practical Guide to Defending Barristers in Disciplinary Cases' by Marc Beaumont
'A Practical Guide to Inherited Wealth on Divorce' by Hayley Trim
'A Practical Guide to Practice Direction 12J and Domestic Abuse in Private Law Children Proceedings' by Rebecca Cross & Malvika Jaganmohan
'A Practical Guide to Confiscation and Restraint' by Narita Bahra QC, John Carl Townsend, David Winch
'A Practical Guide to the Law of Forests in Scotland' by Philip Buchan
'A Practical Guide to Health and Medical Cases in Immigration Law' by Rebecca Chapman & Miranda Butler

'A Practical Guide to Bad Character Evidence for Criminal Practitioners by Aparna Rao
'A Practical Guide to Extradition Law post-Brexit' by Myles Grandison et al
'A Practical Guide to Hoarding and Mental Health for Housing Lawyers' by Rachel Coyle
'A Practical Guide to Psychiatric Claims in Personal Injury – 2nd Edition' by Liam Ryan
'Stephens on Contractual Indemnities' by Richard Stephens
'A Practical Guide to the EU Succession Regulation' by Richard Frimston
'A Practical Guide to Solicitor and Client Costs – 2nd Edition' by Robin Dunne
'Constructive Dismissal – Practice Pointers and Principles' by Benjimin Burgher
'A Practical Guide to Religion and Belief Discrimination Claims in the Workplace' by Kashif Ali
'A Practical Guide to the Law of Medical Treatment Decisions' by Ben Troke
'Fundamental Dishonesty and QOCS in Personal Injury Proceedings: Law and Practice' by Jake Rowley
'A Practical Guide to the Law in Relation to School Exclusions' by Charlotte Hadfield & Alice de Coverley
'A Practical Guide to Divorce for the Silver Separators' by Karin Walker
'The Right to be Forgotten – The Law and Practical Issues' by Melissa Stock
'A Practical Guide to Planning Law and Rights of Way in National Parks, the Broads and AONBs' by James Maurici QC, James Neill et al
'A Practical Guide to Election Law' by Tom Tabori
'A Practical Guide to the Law in Relation to Surrogacy' by Andrew Powell
'A Practical Guide to Claims Arising from Fatal Accidents – 2nd Edition' by James Patience
'A Practical Guide to the Ownership of Employee Inventions – From Entitlement to Compensation' by James Tumbridge & Ashley Roughton
'A Practical Guide to Asbestos Claims' by Jonathan Owen & Gareth McAloon
'A Practical Guide to Stamp Duty Land Tax in England and Northern Ireland' by Suzanne O'Hara
'A Practical Guide to the Law of Farming Partnerships' by Philip Whitcomb
'Covid-19, Homeworking and the Law – The Essential Guide to Employment and GDPR Issues' by Forbes Solicitors
'Covid-19 and Criminal Law – The Essential Guide' by Ramya Nagesh

'Covid-19 and Family Law in England and Wales – The Essential Guide' by Safda Mahmood

'A Practical Guide to the Law of Unlawful Eviction and Harassment – 2nd Edition' by Stephanie Lovegrove

'Covid-19, Brexit and the Law of Commercial Leases – The Essential Guide' by Mark Shelton

'A Practical Guide to Costs in Personal Injury Claims – 2nd Edition' by Matthew Hoe

'A Practical Guide to the General Data Protection Regulation (GDPR) – 2nd Edition' by Keith Markham

'Ellis on Credit Hire – Sixth Edition' by Aidan Ellis & Tim Kevan

'A Practical Guide to Working with Litigants in Person and McKenzie Friends in Family Cases' by Stuart Barlow

'Protecting Unregistered Brands: A Practical Guide to the Law of Passing Off' by Lorna Brazell

'A Practical Guide to Secondary Liability and Joint Enterprise Post-Jogee' by Joanne Cecil & James Mehigan

'A Practical Guide to the Pre-Action RTA Claims Protocol for Personal Injury Lawyers' by Antonia Ford

'A Practical Guide to Neighbour Disputes and the Law' by Alexander Walsh

'A Practical Guide to Forfeiture of Leases' by Mark Shelton

'A Practical Guide to Coercive Control for Legal Practitioners and Victims' by Rachel Horman

'Tackling Disclosure in the Criminal Courts – A Practitioner's Guide' by Narita Bahra QC & Don Ramble

'A Practical Guide to the Law of Driverless Cars – Second Edition' by Alex Glassbrook, Emma Northey & Scarlett Milligan

'A Practical Guide to TOLATA Claims' by Greg Williams

'A Practical Guide to Elderly Law – 2nd Edition' by Justin Patten

'A Practical Guide to Responding to Housing Disrepair and Unfitness Claims' by Iain Wightwick

'A Practical Guide to the Law of Bullying and Harassment in the Workplace' by Philip Hyland

'How to Be a Freelance Solicitor: A Practical Guide to the SRA-Regulated Freelance Solicitor Model' by Paul Bennett

'A Practical Guide to Prison Injury Claims' by Malcolm Johnson

'A Practical Guide to the Small Claims Track – 2nd Edition' by Dominic Bright

'A Practical Guide to Advising Clients at the Police Station' by Colin Stephen McKeown-Beaumont

'A Practical Guide to Antisocial Behaviour Injunctions' by Iain Wightwick

'Practical Mediation: A Guide for Mediators, Advocates, Advisers, Lawyers, and Students in Civil, Commercial, Business, Property, Workplace, and Employment Cases' by Jonathan Dingle with John Sephton

'The Mini-Pupillage Workbook' by David Boyle

'A Practical Guide to Crofting Law' by Brian Inkster

'A Practical Guide to the Law of Domain Names and Cybersquatting' by Andrew Clemson

'A Practical Guide to the Law of Gender Pay Gap Reporting' by Harini Iyengar

'NHS Whistleblowing and the Law' by Joseph England

'Employment Law and the Gig Economy' by Nigel Mackay & Annie Powell

'A Practical Guide to Noise Induced Hearing Loss (NIHL) Claims' by Andrew Mckie, Ian Skeate, Gareth McAloon

'An Introduction to Beauty Negligence Claims – A Practical Guide for the Personal Injury Practitioner' by Greg Almond

'Intercompany Agreements for Transfer Pricing Compliance' by Paul Sutton

'Zen and the Art of Mediation' by Martin Plowman

'A Practical Guide to the SRA Principles, Individual and Law Firm Codes of Conduct 2019 – What Every Law Firm Needs to Know' by Paul Bennett

'A Practical Guide to Adoption for Family Lawyers' by Graham Pegg

'A Practical Guide to Industrial Disease Claims' by Andrew Mckie & Ian Skeate

'A Practical Guide to Redundancy' by Philip Hyland

'A Practical Guide to Vicarious Liability' by Mariel Irvine

'A Practical Guide to Applications for Landlord's Consent and Variation of Leases' by Mark Shelton

'A Practical Guide to Relief from Sanctions Post-Mitchell and Denton' by Peter Causton

'A Practical Guide to Equity Release for Advisors' by Paul Sams

'A Practical Guide to Financial Services Claims' by Chris Hegarty

'The Law of Houses in Multiple Occupation: A Practical Guide to HMO Proceedings' by Julian Hunt

'Occupiers, Highways and Defective Premises Claims: A Practical Guide Post-Jackson – 2nd Edition' by Andrew Mckie
'A Practical Guide to Financial Ombudsman Service Claims' by Adam Temple & Robert Scrivenor
'A Practical Guide to Running Housing Disrepair and Cavity Wall Claims: 2nd Edition' by Andrew Mckie & Ian Skeate
'A Practical Guide to Holiday Sickness Claims – 2nd Edition' by Andrew Mckie & Ian Skeate
'Arguments and Tactics for Personal Injury and Clinical Negligence Claims' by Dorian Williams
'A Practical Guide to Drone Law' by Rufus Ballaster, Andrew Firman, Eleanor Clot
'A Practical Guide to Compliance for Personal Injury Firms Working With Claims Management Companies' by Paul Bennett
'RTA Allegations of Fraud in a Post-Jackson Era: The Handbook – 2nd Edition' by Andrew Mckie
'RTA Personal Injury Claims: A Practical Guide Post-Jackson' by Andrew Mckie
'On Experts: CPR35 for Lawyers and Experts' by David Boyle
'An Introduction to Personal Injury Law' by David Boyle

These books and more are available to order online direct from the publisher at www.lawbriefpublishing.com, where you can also read free sample chapters. For any queries, contact us on 0844 587 2383 or mail@lawbriefpublishing.com.

Our books are also usually in stock at www.amazon.co.uk with free next day delivery for Prime members, and at good legal bookshops such as Wildy & Sons.

We are regularly launching new books in our series of practical day-to-day practitioners' guides. Visit our website and join our free newsletter to be kept informed and to receive special offers, free chapters, etc.

You can also follow us on Twitter at www.twitter.com/lawbriefpub.

www.ingramcontent.com/pod-product-compliance
Lightning Source LLC
LaVergne TN
LVHW022313200926
848481LV00004B/1317
* 9 7 8 1 9 1 6 6 9 8 0 2 4 *